Battle at Sea

CRUISERS

AVERY LEE

BLACK RABBIT BOOKS

Bolt is published by Black Rabbit Books
P.O. Box 227, Mankato, Minnesota, 56002.
www.blackrabbitbooks.com

Alissa Thielges, editor
Jason Knudson, designer

Library of Congress Cataloging-in-Publication Data

Names: Lee, Avery author
Title: Cruisers / Avery Lee.
Description: Mankato, MN: Black Rabbit Books, [2027] | Series: Battle at sea | Includes bibliographical references and index. | Audience: Ages 8-12 | Audience: Grades 4-6
Identifiers: LCCN 2025055128 (print) | LCCN 2025055129 (ebook) | ISBN 9781645826262 library binding | ISBN 9781645828402 paperback | ISBN 9781645826323 ebook
Subjects: LCSH: Cruisers (Warships)—United States—Juvenile literature | CYAC: Cruisers (Warships) | Warships | LCGFT: Instructional and educational works
Classification: LCC V820.3 .L44 2027 (print) | LCC V820.3 (ebook) | DDC 623.825/3—dc23/eng/20260116
LC record available at https://lccn.loc.gov/2025055128

Printed in India

Image Credits

Alamy Stock Photo/AB Forces News Collection, 25; Black Rabbit Books/Jason Knudson, 18, 22–23, 27; DVIDS/Petty Officer 1st Class Rawad Madanat, 10–11; Freepik/freepik, 29, macrovector, 9, macrovector_official, 12, 3D-Horse 22–23; Shutterstock/The Mariner 4291, 28–29; Wikimedia Commons/Commander, U.S. Naval Forces Europe-Africa/U.S. 6th Fleet, 16, Mass Communication Specialist 1st Class Jeremy Graham, 3, 16–17, Mass Communication Specialist 2nd Class Daniel Barker, 9, Mass Communication Specialist 2nd Class Nathan Lockwood, 4–5, MC1 Justin L. Ailes, 21, MC3 Paul Kelly/U.S. Navy, 26–27, National Museum of the U.S. Navy, 1, Naval Surface Warriors, 16, Petty Officer 3rd Class Kevin Cunningham, 6–7, Photographer's Mate 2nd Class Michael Sandberg, 17, Photographer's Mate 3rd Class Bernardo Fuller, 14, Photographer's Mate 3rd Class Lowell Whitman, 24, Photographer's Mate Airman James R. Evans, 19, Photographer's Mate Airman Jordon R. Beesley, 13, 32, Rhk111, 15, Tim Masterson, 16–17, U.S. Naval Forces Central Command/U.S. Fifth Fleet, 7, 17, U.S. Navy/Chief Journalist Joe Kane, cover, 31, United States Navy, 20–21, United States Navy, Mass Communication Specialist John L. Beeman, 21; Every effort has been made to contact copyright holders for material reproduced in this book. Any omissions will be rectified in subsequent printings if notice is given to the publisher.

CONTENTS

CHAPTER 1

Ready for

A U.S. cruiser slices through waves. Its **radar** spins, scanning the skies. Inside, sailors watch glowing screens. Then suddenly, an alert. Enemy ahead!

The **crew** jumps into action. The captain gives orders. Big **missiles** rise from launchers. They move into position. The ship is ready to strike.

Locked and Loaded

The radar locks on. The launcher moves into position. With a roar, a missile blasts skyward. It zooms fast and true. BOOM! It's a hit! **Mission** complete. The cruiser stays strong and steady. It sails on, watchful of other threats.

Some cruisers carry helicopters for rescues.

CHAPTER 2

What Is a

A cruiser is a big warship. The U.S. Navy runs them. They guard other ships and keep oceans safe from enemies. Cruisers are fast. They can travel far without stopping. The radar scans for threats. Guided weapons stop enemy planes and ships. Some can even stop incoming missiles.

567 feet (175 meters)

DESTROYER

610 feet (186 m)

AIRCRAFT CARRIER

1,100 feet (335 m)

PARTS OF A CRUISER

BRIDGE

GUN MOUNT

MISSILE LAUNCHER

HELIPAD

HULL

Better Together

A cruiser might sail alone. More often, it travels with other ships. Cruisers join aircraft carriers and destroyers. They form a group called a **fleet**. A fleet may have two or three cruisers. They guard aircraft carriers. Together, they form a shield at sea.

Life on Board

Days at sea are busy. Crew members share tight living spaces. Meals are served in the mess hall. Sailors work in shifts. Some steer or watch the radar. Others keep the ship running.

When off duty, the crew relaxes. They watch movies or call home. But they stay ready. They can jump back into action quickly.

CREW AT WORK

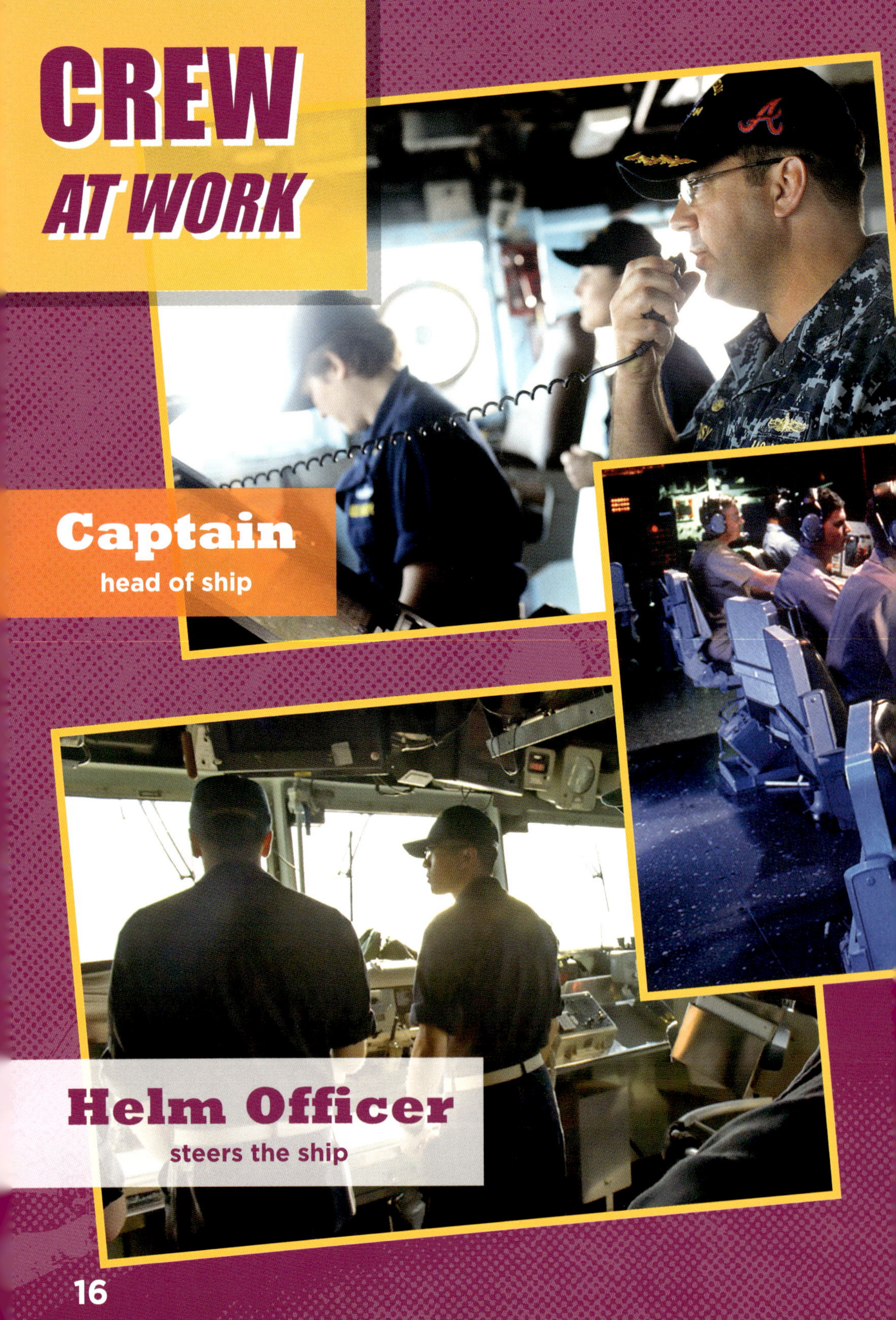

Captain
head of ship

Helm Officer
steers the ship

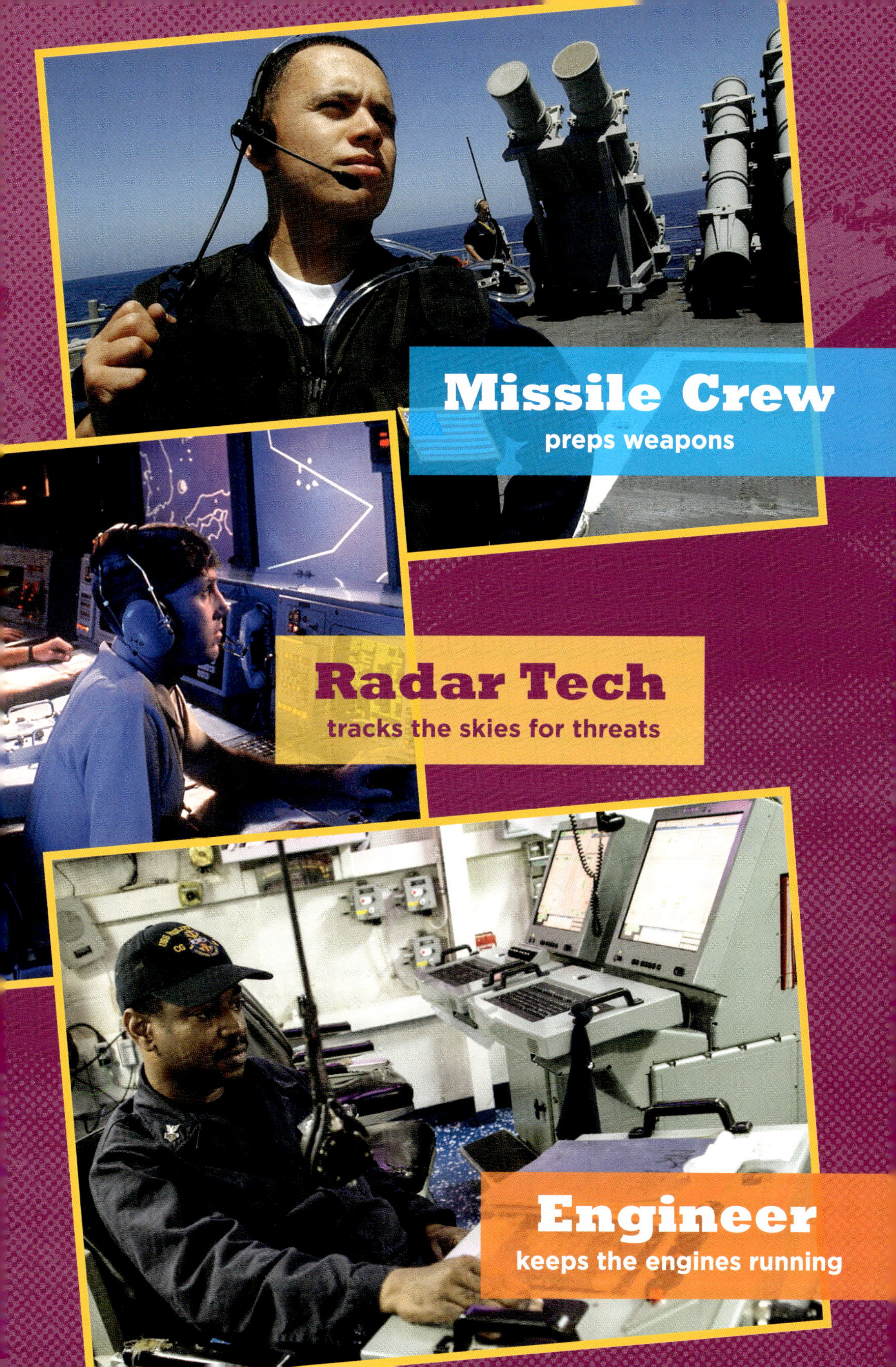
Missile Crew
preps weapons
Radar Tech
tracks the skies for threats
Engineer
keeps the engines running

CHAPTER 3

Powerful

The U.S. Navy only uses one type of cruiser. They are the Ticonderoga class. These ships are built for power and exactness. At their center is AEGIS. This system links radar, computers, and weapons together. It can track more than 100 objects at once.

Destroyers also use this weapon system.

Armed and Ready

Each cruiser packs a lot of missiles. These strike objects in the air and at sea. SM-6s can even hit other missiles in space! Tomahawks are cruise missiles. They are used for long-range strikes. They fly low. Enemies have a hard time seeing them coming.

Weapons on Board

TORPEDOES
Attack submarines.

MISSILES
Attack and sink ships.
Destroy other missiles.

GUNS
Shoot close ships and small, fast boats.
Support for shore missions.

HOW FAR *CAN THEY GO?*

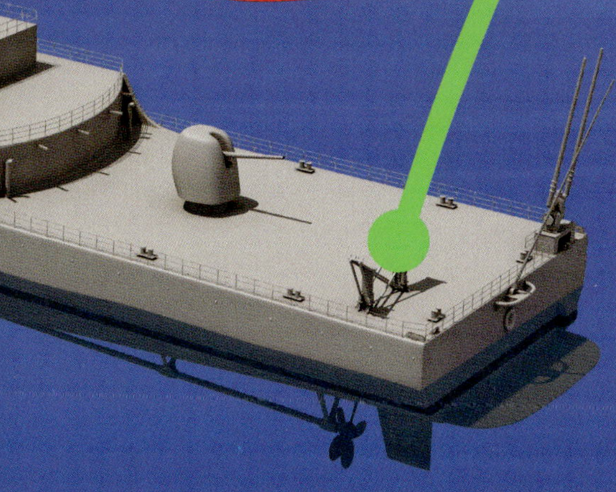

SM-6 missile
230 miles (370 km)
20-mm
Gatling gun
1.9 miles (3 km)
Harpoon
missile
149 miles (240 km)
Mk-46 torpedo
6.2 miles (10 km)

Strong Inside

Inside, the ship is split into sections. If one room gets damaged, doors can close to keep water or fire from spreading. This helps the ship stay afloat. Strong **Kevlar** protects important parts from explosions. If something breaks, backup systems keep the ship running.

CHAPTER 4

Defenders at Sea

Cruisers take on many jobs. They protect fleets from air attacks. They sail nearby to make sure no enemy planes or submarines get too close.

Sometimes, these ships **patrol** dangerous waters. They may guard a **route** to keep it safe for other ships. In peacetime, they help with rescues.

Cruisers have served in many wars.
World War I
World War II
Persian Gulf War
Afghanistan War

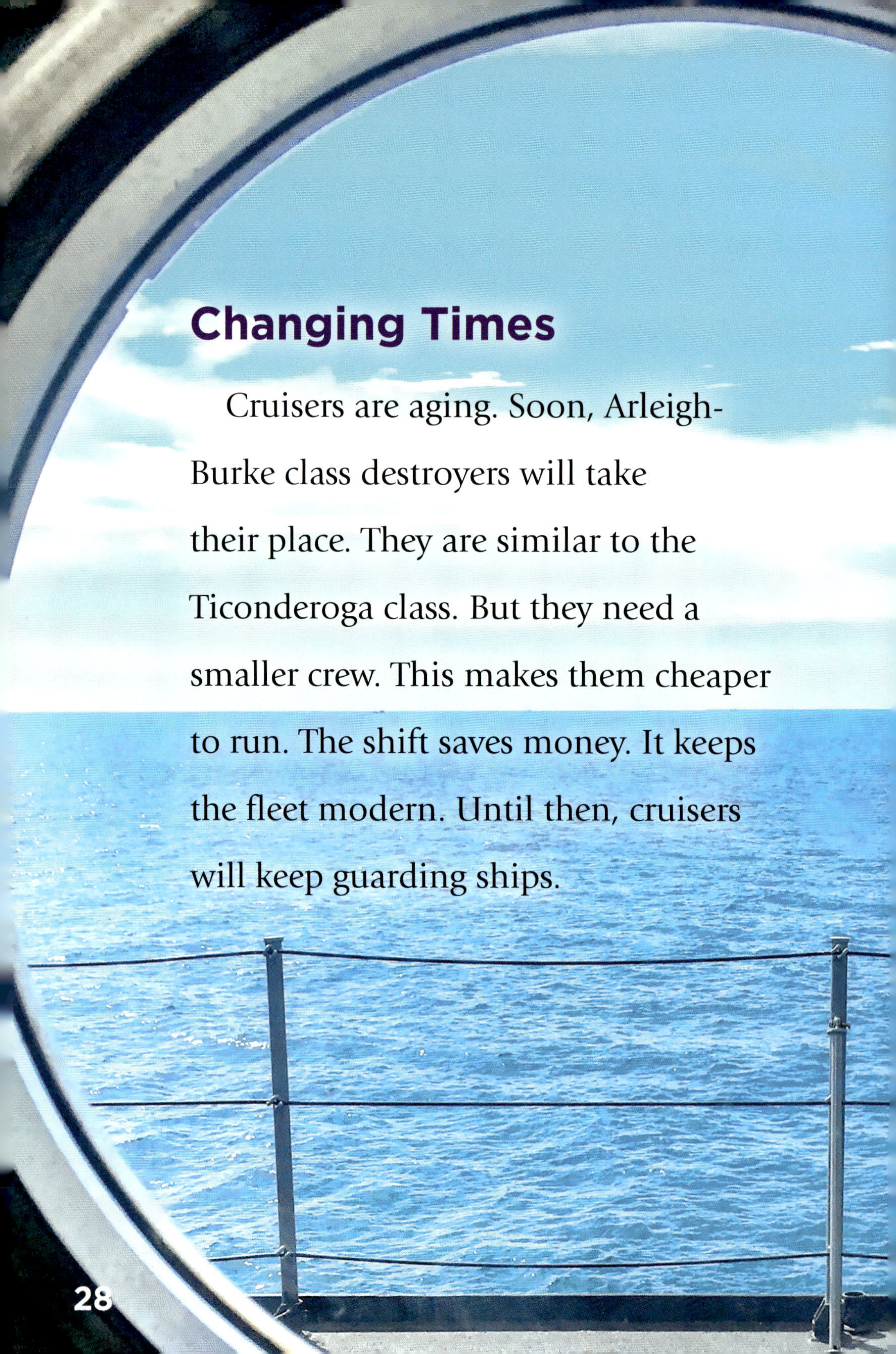

Changing Times

Cruisers are aging. Soon, Arleigh-Burke class destroyers will take their place. They are similar to the Ticonderoga class. But they need a smaller crew. This makes them cheaper to run. The shift saves money. It keeps the fleet modern. Until then, cruisers will keep guarding ships.

35 YEARS
SERVICE
LIFE
OF A
TICONDEROGA CRUISER

GLOSSARY

crew (KROO)—a group of people who operate a machine

fleet (FLEET)—a group of military ships controlled by one leader

Kevlar (KEV-lahr)—a super strong, human-made fabric that can stop things from breaking through

missile (MIS-uhl)—a rocket-powered weapon used for distant targets

mission (MISH-uhn)—a specific military or naval task

patrol (puh-TROHL)—going around an area to make sure it is safe

radar (RAY-dar)—a device that sends out radio waves for finding the location and speed of a moving object

route (ROUT)—the path something takes to get from one place to another

BOOKS

Bolte, Mari. *Warships in Action.* Minneapolis: Lerner Publications, 2024.

McKinney, Donna B. *The United States Navy.* Minneapolis: Bellwether Media, Inc., 2025.

WEBSITES

Cruiser Facts for Kids
kids.kiddle.co/Cruiser

Navy
kids.britannica.com/kids/article/navy/353522

INDEX